Answering the Call
of Creativity

Also by Michele Cassou
Books
Life, Paint and Passion: Reclaiming the Magic of Spontaneous Expression
Point Zero: Creativity without Limits
Kids Play: Igniting Children's Creativity
The Buddhist Art Doctor: Prescriptions for Creative and Non-Creative Seekers
Teachers That Dare: Using the Creative Process to Teach the Creative Process

DVDs
Birth of a Process
Point Zero: Insights and Images
The Flowering of Children's Creativity
Awakening of the Mystic
Body, Sexuality and Spirit

Cover art and illustrations by Michele Cassou
For books, videos, audio, catalogs, or workshop information or to be put on the mailing list, visit Michele's website, www.michelecassou.com.

Copyright © 2016 Michele Cassou
All rights reserved.
ISBN: 1514167492
ISBN-13: 9781514167496
Library of Congress Control Number: 2015908925
CreateSpace Independent Publishing Platform
North Charleston, South Carolina

Answering the Call of Creativity

◆ ◆ ◆

A Radical Approach to the Creative Process through the Discovery of Its Key Principles

Michele Cassou

Contents

The Transcendent Power of Pure Creativity

This Book...

When I teach workshops, I always carry in my painting apron a small notebook and a pen. While I attend to my students, I often have new insights about the creative process, and I like to scribble my discoveries in the little book.

I feel privileged to have witnessed so many creative journeys with their breakthroughs, their bursts of inspiration, and their spirit. Observing this lively process yielding its secrets always inspires me with new enthusiasm, insights, and realizations. As a result, I have filled dozens of notebooks.

Years ago, while visiting me in my home, a young friend noticed a stack of these notebooks on a shelf. Understanding what they were, she exclaimed, "Someday when you stop teaching, we will have to go through all your notes!"

Last year, I happened to remember this comment and suddenly got inspired. "What a good idea!" I thought. "Why not do it right now?"

So I retrieved and typed with great delight those years of lively pointers and organized them into this booklet that I would now like to share with creativity lovers.

Then, over the last few weeks, I felt so inspired by new discoveries about the creative process that I could not help adding a few pages then and there in the book to catch up with the wonder of the present times.

My main creative medium and passion is painting. Readers can substitute other forms of creation where I used the word "painting" since the same principles apply to all creativity.

Michele Cassou

Creativity's deepest purpose is to enter
the unknown of our life
and explore the mystery of being.

Answering the Creative Call

*One gains the power of the river when one swims in
the direction of its flow.*

WU HSIN

All of us humans have a deep urge to touch the source of our being and to manifest our uniqueness, but our minds lead us astray with expectations, preferences, beliefs, and conditioning.

To answer the Creative Call, we need to see how simple and natural creativity is and how it works. We need to discover its basic principles and its natural laws. These new understandings will inspire us to step out of the established tracks and help us go beyond a mind that is afraid to break into new ground.

We can then free ourselves from self-made or inherited limitations and soar into infinite possibilities. When we answer the Creative Call, we can never go back to old molds and models. We find the authentic self and its passion to create.

◆ ◆ ◆

How often do we feel our hunger to create? We might choose to ignore its pull, but it's always there, waiting and trying to attract our attention.

That hunger to create is a call to express who we are with authenticity, abandon, and integrity.

To create intuitively is to become
a true pioneer of the heart.

The Radical Power
of the Principles of Creativity

Roots wither in the darkness.
Keeping the root healthy and
well watered
will insure that the fruits are sweet.
Attention should always be
directed to the root.
WU HSIN

The Principles of Creativity offer a solid and inspiring ground to stand on when we create. They hold the magic key to layers of exploration into the depth of our beings.

Often when people think they are creatively blocked or lack talent, they might simply be carrying a misconception about creativity and its potential.

When the true purpose of creativity is rediscovered and understood, anyone can answer the creative call.

Becoming familiar with the Principles *transforms* the way we create. It helps us uncover the way creation actually works, and the need to struggle vanishes as we enter process.

We instinctively move away from criticism and the drive for product.

We learn to paint for ourselves as *intuition* and *spontaneity* become the main propelling factors of our inspiration.

If you do not grab and cling to the known,
the unknown will find you.

The Amazing Role
of the Principles of Creativity

*Pure creativity does not give you
what you want;
it gives you what you need.*

M. C.

Among other gifts, the principles of creativity

- bring **authenticity** to the work,
- stimulate **self-expression** and self-discovery,
- activate **liveliness and presence** of Being,
- keep **inspiration** flowing,
- break through **creative blocks**,
- allow us to explore the **unconscious** mind,
- **heal** emotional wounds,
- yield **insights** and wisdom,
- generate **confidence** and strength in one's creative potential,
- light an endless exploration into **the spirit**.

The principles of creativity move artists of all kinds away from negative criticism and toward a positive creative response, allowing them to see the boundless space beyond right and wrong, success and failure, honesty and manipulation.

A Clue to Creativity
Rules versus Principles

Pure water only flows from a pure source.
WU HSIN

Differentiating between rules and principles is a major key to finding creative power and its lasting inspiration.

1. **Principles are very different from rules.**

   A rule is based on the idea of good or bad, success or failure. It is a man-made decision based on a technique, a theory, or a strategy.

   Rules and techniques vary with the beliefs and inclinations of the person who develops them. They are subjective and limited. They are stored and used by the mind only in the *specific way* for which they were designed. They show what to do and where to go and how to proceed, leaving very little space for true expression.

2. **A principle of creativity is a natural law.**

   Principles of creativity expand on the way nature moves. These principles stand true no matter the situation, the creation, or the person.

   They offer a sturdy ground for creativity, giving painters *the means and freedom to follow their intuition and spontaneity.* The principles aim beyond thinking and are naturally oriented to reach the heart in its wisdom.

Intuition is wild and unpredictable.

Key Principles
Nourishing Your Creative Potential

The creative principles are in harmony
with the working of the universe.
Wisdom, common sense, and spirit dwell within them.

M. C.

No need to be inspired, gifted,
or talented to create.
The life force in you is immensely creative;
nothing needs to be added to it.

True creative inspiration arises from a pure place,
the source and heart of intuition.
Intuition comes from a place of
no conditioning, no agenda, and no planning.
It does not rely on the thinking process
and moves only in the now, regardless of preferences.

Creativity asks you to stop moving in patterns
and to STEP OUT of conditioned ideas
that control how you act
and evaluate and judge your work.
It asks you to be open and spontaneous.

◆ ◆ ◆

Creative intuition has a fierce and daring job;
it destroys the projections and prejudices
that color and deform your world
in millions of ways.
It frees you.

◆ ◆ ◆

Imagination comes from the mind,
intuition from the source,
from the Point Zero that is always present.
Intuition flows naturally out of you
when you forget to think.

◆ ◆ ◆

The intuitive energy of creativity arises spontaneously,
joining its personal flow to the universal.
This greater stream reveals and explores many levels
of feelings, sensations, perceptions, and spiritual dimensions.

◆ ◆ ◆

Creativity is a process.
The creative process is about unlearning,
letting go of rules and models,
destroying the false,
the borrowed,
the believed,
the expected.
It is about entering
PRESENCE.

◆ ◆ ◆

Creative integrity is a Roto-Rooter
for stuck,
denied,
hidden,
or unfinished feelings,
giving them the freedom to move and express.

◆ ◆ ◆

The intuitive process of creativity takes away what you are not,
what is not yours, what you do not need, and nothing else.
The unnecessary is instinctively washed away by intuition.
What you truly are and have cannot be stolen from you.
Creative freedom, by allowing you to inhabit yourself,
breaks the false boundaries of who you think you are
and brings you back to Being.

◆ ◆ ◆

Intuitive painting happens in the NOW!
Painting for a projected product equals
painting for a fictional future.

◆ ◆ ◆

The act of inventing is never
an act of reproducing, copying, or manipulating.
It moves like the wind, going its own way.

◆ ◆ ◆

Life cannot be infused into a canvas
by manipulating colors and shapes.
It can manifest spontaneously
only when you get out of the way.

❖ ❖ ❖

Respect what has been born naturally.
What appears spontaneously out of a painter's brush
always deserves respect and a nonjudgmental approach.

❖ ❖ ❖

Creative painting expresses itself in two ways:
abstract forms
and images.
Both are natural;
no need to start a fight between the two.

❖ ❖ ❖

Playfulness, liveliness, and presence
feed the fire of creativity.

❖ ❖ ❖

Creativity is what happens when there is
harmony between you and your work.
To create is to open up and surrender to what is.
It requires a state of nonavoidance
of feelings and sensations,
of not labeling or evaluating.

◆ ◆ ◆

In creativity the focus is on the person,
not on the outcome.
What matters when you create is the inner urge
to express and explore,
NOT the shape it takes.

◆ ◆ ◆

Creativity is a powerful vehicle
to explore what you deeply feel and who you truly are.

◆ ◆ ◆

**When painting has no set destination
but is moved by the desire to explore,
painters become *pioneers* in this mysterious
universe.**

◆ ◆ ◆

The goal of the creator is to LET GO
of external teachings and models
and find authentic inspiration.

The Product Trap
Creativity as Process

When the mind is seen as
continually kidnapped by thoughts,
the first stop toward freedom has been taken.
WU HSIN

Creative intuition, when you listen to it,
makes everything bloom.
It is the voice of the heart.
It explores the unknown,
the unexpected,
and the deeply felt.
It holds the power to transform your work
in ways you cannot imagine.

◆ ◆ ◆

Developing your intuition
is a crucial step in the creative process.
Creation beyond thinking is practiced for
the experience and the exploration of the unknown
as opposed to a thinking imagination
that keeps you roaming in the mental fields of the past.

◆ ◆ ◆

The creative process loves the unexpected.
If you lose your creative freedom and its gifts,
you become a slave
of appearances and results.
You move away from the fluidity,
the flow, and the joy of a live process.

◆ ◆ ◆

Creative intuition does not hold any agendas.
Watch for your acquired tendency
to generate rules and techniques,
building a cage around yourself.

◆ ◆ ◆

To remove the cork blocking your creativity,
do not take refuge in your knowing mind,
but roam into the mystery of your life.

◆ ◆ ◆

There are no mistakes in creativity.
Each step is necessary to the unfolding of freedom;
a small detour is not a failure
but a gestation time
or a preparation
for the intensity of a journey into the unknown.

No need to study and learn to create intuitively.
In freedom your innocence and enthusiasm
will find the way for what they must express
and how to do it,
breathing life into your creations.

◆ ◆ ◆

Pure creativity has no limitations.
Remember to keep your images alive, strange, surprising,
and unexpected in proportions, colors, and expressions.
Do not keep them on a leash!

◆ ◆ ◆

The natural flow of the creative process
can always be trusted.
Attempting to correct and perfect an intuitive expression
is like trying to reshape and redecorate a wildflower.

◆ ◆ ◆

The intuitive process spontaneously births
out of you the new and the authentic.
If you don't cling to a specific result,
images, colors, and shapes
will appear on their own
to your astonishment and delight.

◆ ◆ ◆

Pure creativity induces a shift from thinking to being.
Your willingness to drop your attachment
to product and its thoughts
will propel you far from superficial outcomes
and into a land of discoveries.

◆ ◆ ◆

Pure process bears no conflict.
When you judge your painting,
you fight with it;
actually, you
start a *war* with yourself.
Remember, there is a potent place beyond criticism.

◆ ◆ ◆

True process moves you beyond the good and the bad.
Have you ever asked yourself,
Why am I so attached to liking my painting?
Can you see that liking or disliking
imprisons you in the world of opposites?
Is it what you really want?

◆ ◆ ◆

Intuition expresses its freedom in wide spaces
where judgments, evaluations, and expectations
do not reach, transcending *duality*.

Trust your intuition;
dare to listen to it and take risks.
See what it can do for you
when you pay attention to its call.

◆ ◆ ◆

Creative intuition ignores the mind's demands.
Your conditioned minds,
left to themselves,
control your creations
in terms of success and failure,
gaining and losing,
always looking for an ego's full meal.

◆ ◆ ◆

Creativity gives form to the invisible;
it invents or reinvents its own images.
For instance, painting a body can be scary
if you think you have to portray
a physical and emotional resemblance,
but not if you follow your wild, spontaneous instinct.

◆ ◆ ◆

Creativity is moved by integrity and humility.
What you paint does not have
to be beautiful,
proportional,
balanced,
or meaningful to your eyes,
just honest and truthful.

◆ ◆ ◆

Beauty is harmony between you and your work.
Did you forget
that true beauty
is the *only* thing
that can come out of you naturally?

◆ ◆ ◆

Practice being where you already are.
There is nowhere else to go.
Inhabit the present moment
one stroke of paint at a time...
It is so simple!

◆ ◆ ◆

Questions to Ponder

~ When you create, do you want entertainment or exploration?

~ Is your mind in a creative mode or in a business mode?

~ Are you trying to gain something or give of yourself?

◆ ◆ ◆

One More Pointer

Imagination and Intuition

Intuition is often confused with imagination, but they are quite different. Imagination is a response from the content of our accumulated thoughts from the big thinking warehouse. It is the capacity to come up with various ideas that rearrange the past in new ways. It cannot add a truly fresh element or a deeper level because it is limited and enclosed within the boundaries of what has already been experienced and thought of.

On the other hand, intuition rises from the unknown. It passes through us freely, propelling us beyond expectations and enticing ideas. Intuition dwells in the depths of the present moment.

WATCH OUT for
the Lurking, Pleasure-Seeking,
Controlling Thief
of Creativity!

Freedom or Control
Intuition versus Planning

It is only through losing one's mind
that one may come to one's senses.
All else is like trying to smooth water.
Wu Hsin

Images are always on their way to being expressed.
They flow with life;
they ceaselessly knock on your door.
All we need
is to open the door and welcome them,
no matter what they are.

Creativity is an instant response.
The present moment connects you
with the whole of life
and manifests through intuition.
Why push it away? Or dissect it?
Or manipulate it? Or question it?
The present moment is born in its own perfection.

♦ ♦ ♦

Creativity does not need you to come up
with clever ideas, symbols, themes,
or special texture on your spontaneous creations.
Let them grow and evolve naturally.
Why not be intrigued by the images, forms, and colors
that appear all of a sudden like magic?
Watch them grow, and let them *take you* on their journey.

◆ ◆ ◆

Creative intuition never asks, "What's next?"
Dormant seeds do not need your efforts
and your planning to sprout and bloom.
Every form, if you let it, grows naturally
to its full expression and ripeness.

◆ ◆ ◆

Process or control?
In the creative process, the first question to ask is,
am I coming from an open and willing place
or from a controlling and rigid one?

◆ ◆ ◆

Creativity does not come from thinking.
The attempts to manipulate the outcome
manifest in many ways and can escape your attention,
especially when feelings are confused with thinking
and reality is confused with projections.
Let's pay attention to *who* is painting.

◆ ◆ ◆

Vulnerability is the main companion to creativity.
To enter the creative state,
you need to unzip your inner being
and stand inwardly naked and vulnerable,
refusing self-protection.

♦ ♦ ♦

The unexpected always flows in the pure creative act.
If you want to invite the unknown,
make yourself ready in your heart
to be kneaded like dough
by this mysterious, wise, and intuitive energy of creation.

♦ ♦ ♦

On the creative path, intuition and spontaneity
move you far from your common wants;
you become fluid and open
to the unfamiliar,
the strange,
the beyond…

♦ ♦ ♦

The stop sign to creative energy: wanted product.
When you plan your creation,
struggles and judgments are bound
to haunt and torment you for not matching your goal.
Rather, experiment with the thrill of the adventure
of letting your work move on its own two feet.

Imagination will make you veer from your true path.
The price to pay for creative passion is
renouncing and letting go of
an imagined, well-planned product.

◆ ◆ ◆

Do not take success and failure as your own doing.
They are just stories in the head!
Let them be and move on.

◆ ◆ ◆

The purpose of self-expression is
to let happen
what is already happening.

◆ ◆ ◆

The seeds of all possible expressions
are inside you.
They will flower in their own time.
No need to rush or force nature.
Welcome what comes NOW!

◆ ◆ ◆

Your creativity flows best when your mind is most silent.
It's impossible to think and follow your intuition at the same time.
You cannot drink from two sources at once
and quench your thirst.

◆ ◆ ◆

Thinking knowledge versus being knowledge
Your thinking knowledge
about what you should do
imprisons you.
Your being knowledge
frees you.

◆ ◆ ◆

Intuition is not choosing,
but responding
to an inner intimation.

◆ ◆ ◆

To enter the creative process is to welcome the unfamiliar
and find the courage to safely cross the lines
set by others
or yourself.

◆ ◆ ◆

Spontaneity and intuition are the powerful
vehicles of the creative process.

◆ ◆ ◆

The gift of authenticity
Watch how hard it is, in the long run,
to NOT DO what is
truly authentic!
In the end you always lose.

❖ ❖ ❖

Intuition is the underlying muse of every moment,
a grace that manifests in the subtlest ways.
It cannot be packaged
or used at will.

❖ ❖ ❖

Personal or universal creativity?
Don't confuse imagination and intuition.
Imagination is from the mind, limited to its storage.
Intuition is a natural, spontaneous voice
fueled by universal energy.

◆ ◆ ◆

You do not need to believe what you tell yourself
about your work!
The commenting and evaluating words
you hear in your head come from rambling
and stubborn conditioning.

◆ ◆ ◆

If you paint just what you want,
you only paint what you know.
The new eludes you, and you find yourself
endlessly turning in circles.

Questions to Ponder

～ Are you following a plan or riding on your intuition?

～ Do you resist or dread spontaneity?

～ Are you sure you want to discard the next spontaneous step? Do you know any better?

～ Are you surfing the wave of creative intuition or telling yourself endless stories?

～ Are you getting tired of your plans and their demands? Are you not weary of putting your future in shackles?

◆ ◆ ◆

More Pointers

Discover how the thinking mind can push away intuition.
You could, for instance, manipulate the size, shape, appearance, or color of your spontaneous images.

You also could give a meaning to your work and keep everything consistent while intuition asks for other things.

You could label the mood of the painting or give it a title and stay enclosed within it, afraid to move, lest you change it. Be aware: there are many ways to abandon the intuitive process.

When you choose your next brush strokes, you might be caught in the rigid net of the wanted result.

The True Voice of Intuition
Creativity beyond Thinking

As a society we have been brought up using our thoughts for everything we do, work for, and feel; so much so that when we experience the world, our experience passes through our thoughts, which control and interpret them. *We have now learned to feel and create with our heads!* What we think influences, colors, and deforms reality because we see through our thought projections. They are like screens that filter, rearrange, and manipulate what we perceive in order to make it acceptable and pleasurable and fit into our lives.

There is nothing wrong with the thinking process when it is in its proper place: a practical tool in daily life and for technology and all sorts of inventions. But when we talk about creativity, the thinking process loses its privileged place, and *we have to rely on another source beyond thinking*. This is when we discover intuition and its crucial and potent role.

Pure creativity is sourced by intuition. Intuition is a spontaneous, natural voice that arises when thinking and its demands are absent. The space of non-thinking opens a gateway for intuition and creativity to manifest through and allows spontaneous expression and exploration of the mystery of living. Intuition passes through the whole of our Being, heart, gut, mind, and spirit. It sources before the thinking mind takes over, before conditioning is set, before we can remember, organize, or plan our next move. Intuition is a purely spontaneous event, and it moves without conflict, naturally and faithfully.

The voice of intuition has great power and intelligence. Born out of the meeting between the energy of the universe and the personal self, it reveals the hidden and the beyond. By not letting us plan, ignore, or manipulate our spontaneity, intuition propels us out of our usual tracks and into the unknown of life. It frees us from past conditioning by taking us to an expanded level of Being. In that new context, concepts, expectations, and fixed patterns cannot rule us anymore because they are part of a small sense of self, which does not reflect our true reality.

Intuition blooms when we surrender to the moment, face the void, and open fully to the unknown. Then, the potential of creativity opens its doors wide and pours its mystery into our work. Intuition reveals what we could not have thought of or imagined. It creates from beyond the boundaries of the imaginable.

Intuition flows spontaneously out of us when we forget to think and we surrender to the energy of presence.

The non-thinking state is a drastic break from the traditional attitude that works with self-interest, rules, techniques, and control.

This experience of pure intuition is so unique and powerful that it cannot be described; it has to be lived. The first time it is discovered is like receiving an initiation or being struck by a flash of lightning or making an amazing discovery.

Before pure creativity is fully experienced, creators-to-be often confuse being excited over an idea with being in the deep flow of the creative process. To truly develop creativity, one cannot compromise. *The slightest compromise chases intuition away* and reverts the energy to the thinking process. The thinking process, desperate not to lose its power, attempts by all means to keep its influence and offers creators crumbs and clever concepts to keep their work going.

To truly understand intuition is a dramatic and astonishing event. Its deeper purpose is to express, explore, and reveal not only the realms of feelings (conscious and unconscious) but also the spiritual dimensions of our lives. Ultimately the intuitive creative process leads us to discover who we truly are. The non-thinking approach opens a space that allows insights and revelations to enter our consciousness and reacquaint us with Being.

◆ ◆ ◆

Thinking is the greatest obstacle to pure creativity.

When you judge your painting,
you fight with it.
Actually, you start a war with yourself.

Creative Blocks
Why Struggle?

Expectation is the grandfather of
disappointment.
The world can never
own a man
that wants nothing.
                    WU HSIN

Creativity will find your blocks wherever they are.
It knows where to go to crack you open
and revive you with new passion.

Creative blocks are intelligent manifestations
of the creative process trying to reorient you
in the direction most suited
to your soul.

Blocks appear when feelings pull you in one direction
and the mind somewhere else.

◆ ◆ ◆

Creative blocks are *hidden agendas or beliefs*
trying to force their way against
the flow of feelings and the needs of the moment.

◆ ◆ ◆

There is always a way through creative blocks.
Bring the light of understanding to them.
No need to fight their darkness.
Let them deliver their messages.

◆ ◆ ◆

Creative blocks are built unconsciously.
They appear when you try to force into the work
something that does not belong there:

- an idea, an image
- a desire for product, for meaning
- a desire for resolution

They are calling you back to the real you.

◆ ◆ ◆

The purpose of creative blocks is
to open new doors
by breaking the resistance
to what you truly feel and are.

◆ ◆ ◆

Creative blocks develop
when you struggle with
who you think you are
and what you expect to become.

◆ ◆ ◆

Nothing can release a creative block
except
a true movement
toward yourself.

◆ ◆ ◆

True Skill
Be more eager to develop
the skill of following your genuine inspiration
rather than the skill of techniques and control.

◆ ◆ ◆

Obstacles
What is authentic and beautiful in you
flows and grows
when obstacles to intuition
are removed
and creativity is understood.

◆ ◆ ◆

Permission
Judgments and criticisms point out
where you are closing the door to your creativity
with lack of *permission*
and acceptance.

The best medicine for creative blocks
When there is discomfort, do not run from it.
Welcome it!
Go toward it!
Embrace it!

Flattery in the creative work
If creativity is used to flatter your self-image,
your work will most likely backfire on you.

You only get trapped
when you are following an agenda or a goal.
Hypnotized by the desire for a special result,
you are kept a prisoner.
Remember, you are holding the key to your freedom.

◆ ◆ ◆

Blocks are an urgent warning
that you have more to explore and risk.
They are incentives and requests
for you to listen to your intuition
and surrender to the creative road!

◆ ◆ ◆

Security in the creative process
Enjoy the meaningful security of moving
with your spontaneous intuition
rather than with clever and self-serving ideas.

◆ ◆ ◆

A creative block is both a locked door
and a key,
depending on how you use it.

◆ ◆ ◆

Questions to Ponder

〜 What would you paint if you could risk ruining everything?

〜 What would you paint if you were not afraid to be inconsistent? Inappropriate? Wild? Outrageous? If you were not afraid to paint chaos?

〜 What would you paint if you had no fear of mistakes?

◆ ◆ ◆

More Pointers

~ Impossible creative questions have the power to propel you into the creative space.
They force you out of your thoughts because the mind cannot answer them. That is their amazing power.
These questions aim at a hidden part of you in order to shake it and wake it up.

~ For more suggestions and examples of questions, please consult the *Questions* booklet that you will find at www.michelecassou.com.

Let Creativity expand your world
and make your life *VIBRATE*
with *new dimensions* of being.

Creative Discomfort
Its Wisdom and Rewards

Nothing succeeds like failure.
Failure is a natural
call for attention like pain.
To pay attention is to step out of your trance.
WU HSIN

Discomfort is a precious pointer.
Surrendering to it guides you to discover
the obstacles to your vulnerability.

◆ ◆ ◆

Discomfort comes from resisting
What needs to be done next.
It is the stirring of the new
asking you to surrender to
the mysterious movement of life.

◆ ◆ ◆

Expectation of results is
the past put in pictures
and projected into the future.
The worms of decay are already eating at it
while the mind, never satisfied,
complains from lack of interest.

◆ ◆ ◆

Discomfort is a friendly messenger
pointing toward the essential reality;
welcome and respect it in order to hear its message.
Don't question the process; question your *openness!*

◆ ◆ ◆

When you go beyond your comfort zone,
intuition unearths feelings you were unaware of.
As a result, resistance builds and causes uneasiness.
If this is faced, the benevolent power of creativity
will lead you to heal the unwanted stress and learn from it.

◆ ◆ ◆

Creative intuition can express what has been
denied, repressed, or avoided,
whether conscious or unconscious.
It has the capacity to reveal all feelings,
from the most raw to the most subtle.

◆ ◆ ◆

Creative seeds know how to grow.
Try stepping out of their way
by letting go of your moods and wants,
no matter how challenging they seem.

◆ ◆ ◆

Tiredness and stress might set in when
you are moving away from what you feel.
To find the core of your creative potential,
all you need is to surrender to *what is.*

◆ ◆ ◆

Opportunities
When the painting seems ruined,
there is nothing to lose anymore!
Use that unique chance
to be fully free
and dare to take risks.

◆ ◆ ◆

Crossing lines or breaking taboos
can feel threatening to your self-image.
If you do cross taboo lines, congratulate yourself!
Your intuition is getting stronger
than your fears!

Avoid being trapped by the rule of consistency.
Up to the last instant of your creative work,
you have *complete freedom* for anything to happen.
You do not have to finish the way you started.
Often, amazing surprises or insights
reveal themselves at the very last moment.

◆ ◆ ◆

Feeling embarrassed when you create is a good omen!
It means you have gone beyond prejudices
and your intuition has freed itself
from your fearful thoughts.
You have left the no-risk area for truly new ground.
You are on your way to discovery.

◆ ◆ ◆

No need to fear criticism.
If people react to your creations and judge them,
it's obviously their problem,
never yours.
Being triggered by your images shows
that they need to face them in themselves.

◆ ◆ ◆

When you create from a small mind,
you can feel quite lonely and uncertain,
but that loneliness evaporates without fail
when your intuition merges
with the universal stream.

◆ ◆ ◆

Natural creativity is a benevolent,
healing, and intelligent process.
Watch it at work; see its magical qualities,
and learn to trust it.

When it is there,
let the discomfort be alive and kicking!
It stimulates and energizes your creative response.

Questions to Ponder

~ During creative struggles ask yourself, who is fighting whom?

~ Are you moving in the creative process NOW or dealing with mental concepts?

~ What would you do if you did not have to protect yourself?

~ What would you do if you did not know what to do in a special area that is left empty? What could be done?

◆ ◆ ◆

More Pointers

~ When in doubt, ask yourself a large encompassing question such as, could anything appear spontaneously anywhere? **But do not answer with your head!**

~ Ask questions that do not talk to or stimulate your mind! Listen to your heart, guts, and soul. Be honest with yourself.

~ If you have a doubt about the next step, do not force anything. Something new is preparing itself to be born in you, right now, unknown to you. Let it grow. Don't rush.

~ When confused, go back to the whole and re-enter yourself.

On Finishing
Reaching Deeper into Yourself

Don't cut a flower before it gives its seed
if you want the next season to flourish.
Let the painting give birth to its many children.

◆ ◆ ◆

Never rush the ending.
It would leave you in an unformed, cutoff space
where it would be hard to start again and find inspiration.

◆ ◆ ◆

How can you know when you are finished
if you don't know
where you are going?
Think about that!

◆ ◆ ◆

Complete your painting carefully,
not because you have to
but because you are following
the thread of a gold mine in yourself.

◆ ◆ ◆

Dare and risk! Do not worry about going too far!
You cannot lose what is truly yours.

◆ ◆ ◆

Creative freedom takes away only what you do not need.
So give yourself to it;
make love with it and enjoy its embrace.
Remember, you are painting on a simple sheet of paper or canvas;
you are not dealing with a life-and-death issue!

◆ ◆ ◆

The biggest obstacle to creativity is good taste.
PABLO PICASSO

Questions to Ponder

~ What would I do next if I was not afraid to go too far?

~ What would I do if anything could come *out of a very precise place* in an image or shape already created? (Most important question!)

~ What would I paint if I were not afraid to ruin my painting? This does not mean that you have to ruin your work. You are only looking for free inspiration and learning how to dare.

~ What would I create if I had no fear of mistakes?

◆ ◆ ◆

More Pointers

~ You can never know when you are fully finished since you are moving in the unknown. You can only question and be willing. Check your creative energy.

~ Remember that the ending is often the more important time in your work. During the ending you have the option to go beyond everything you can think of and to still reach deeper.

~ Your next creative work will start at the intutitive level where you finished your last work. A well-finished work fertilizes the birth of your next creation.

◆ ◆ ◆

If you do not define and interpret
your feelings,
your attention will *GO TOWARD BEING.*

Meaning versus Insight
Interpretation and Its Side Effects

Like a spider spinning its web,
painters wrap meaning and stories
around their work.
These stories churn in their heads,
signaling the end of adventure,
the end of genuine creativity.
The painters then
follow only one narrow track:
their stories' track.

M. C.

The painting process stimulates insights.
Insights are a spontaneous realization from the heart,
a burst of wisdom that comes directly from intuition.
Insights happen when your creations are not manipulated
but follow the principles of nature.
When intuitive purity reaches a profound level,
insights rise to the surface.

Although insights come from
the vast space of not knowing,
interpretations come from what you already know,
only rearranged.

◆ ◆ ◆

Stories and interpretations about your work,
about how good or bad your creations are,
and about what they mean
act as *wet cement*:
you put your feet in it, and soon you can't move.

◆ ◆ ◆

The painting process is not about
painting what you think you feel;
it is about feeling and painting.
Anything else is dealing with the past
and is controlled by mental constructs.

◆ ◆ ◆

If you do not explain your paintings to yourself,
insights are then free to arise
and will pop up
and surprise and amaze you with their wisdom.

◆ ◆ ◆

When you attach meaning to a spontaneous image,
you enclose it in a tight space and
it becomes a **hostage with a label.**

The creative process is not about following a feelings map
or resolving psychological problems.
(Though there is a significant therapeutic effect.)
It is about bringing authenticity to your life
and becoming an avid explorer of new lands,
a true pioneer of heart and soul.

◆ ◆ ◆

Everything you think about your painting is irrelevant.
When it's time to know something,
an insight will appear naturally.
No need to search for it.

◆ ◆ ◆

It is so refreshing and enlivening
to let go of interpretations
and find a moment of innocence.

◆ ◆ ◆

Inside each of us there is
a storage of unfinished and repressed feelings.
These emotional pockets,
which hold pain and darkness,
are spontaneously brought to the surface
when creativity is unleashed.
They have raw intensity
and need to be expressed boldly and freely
without being defined by our interpretations.
Each release is a beautiful and wise experience,
an awakening.

◆ ◆ ◆

If you put your feelings into a clever idea
or a rigid concept or just disguise them
to avoid being vulnerable,
you compromise your depth of expression
and the sharp wisdom of creativity vanishes.

◆ ◆ ◆

Spontaneous expression is never dangerous.
If any danger exists, it would be
to not paint what intuition gives you!
Then, the images might stay inside you,
turning round and round,
like a monkey in a cage,
until the end of times.

◆ ◆ ◆

The temptation to interpret,
to judge, or to comment on your creation
risks killing its sacred connection
with deeper truth.

◆ ◆ ◆

The images of your creations dance
the joyful dance of the opposites
only to establish a footstep beyond both.

There is nothing to prove or resolve;
just be in the moment.
Let everything evolve and transform
with the benevolent wisdom of intuition.

Stories about what you have created
can lure you
because they entertain you
but mostly because they solidify
and feed your ego.

The only thing your thinking can do when you create
is to superimpose itself upon what intuition already gave you.
If you listen to your thoughts,
the gold thread of an authentic process is lost.

Don't believe what you tell yourself about your work.
These inside voices are old recordings
borrowed and rehearsed many times.
The mind that has been in control for so long
does not want to lose its power;
it is afraid of the unfamiliar, the different, and the new,
and is attempting to stop it by chattering endlessly.

If you take the content of your painting *literally*,
you are missing the greater gift of the creative process:
its ongoing potential of healing and revelations.

Images express immense mysteries, most of them invisible.
Images are only 5 percent of what they seem to be;
the other 95 percent is invisible to the naked eye.
Surrender to that transcendent principle
and let yourself wonder.

Be aware of the seductive power of meaning.
Looking for meaning in your painting
could swallow you in the blink of an eye,
dry up your intuition, and steal your inspiration.
Watch for the active thief of creativity!

It is who you think you are at that moment
who does the interpreting, no one else!
Your load of used-up thoughts is offering you
a secondhand thought to add to your large storage.
Truth and realization lay far beyond the confines of the mind.

◆ ◆ ◆

Letting go of the meaning of what you create
is coming back to the source of being, to your essence,
to the point before conditioning took place,
the point zero in yourself.

◆ ◆ ◆

If you have a reason to do something, it's not spontaneous.
Listen to the body's energy instead,
and follow its lead.

The point is never to find a meaningful image to paint
or to resolve a problem,
but to enter the process with simplicity and joy.

◆ ◆ ◆

Questions to Ponder

~ Ask yourself, why am I refusing to feel what I am feeling now? Do I really know better? *Or did the universe make a mistake?*

~ How would it feel to paint without being a character in the story of your painting but rather an explorer of an unknown world?

~ Why do you think you need to interpret your painting?

~ Why do you insist on keeping your beliefs of what "should" happen?

~ Are you a captive audience of your thinking, your judgment, and your interpretations?

◆ ◆ ◆

More Pointers

〜 If you do not interpret your feelings, insights will come to you on their own.

〜 Intutition gives you what you need, not what you want or expect. It is always more powerful and surprising than what you could have imagined.

〜 True realizations are born in your heart and guts when you create and will move last to your mind. You cannot force or rush them.
They obey a wise and natural current.

◆ ◆ ◆

**Do you follow everything you create
with a comment, a critique, or an explanation?**

**What can you expect from that conditioned
commentator?**

Think about that!

◆ ◆ ◆

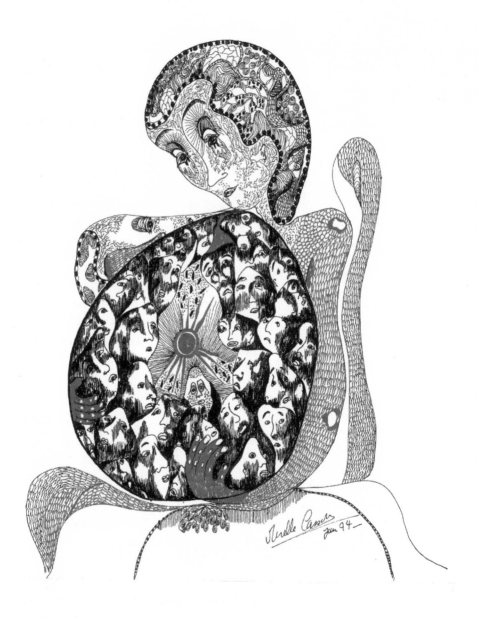

The Power of the Raw Feeling

When pure intuition guides our creativity, we become inwardly open and vulnerable, and we travel in the mysterious unknown. We switch from a conditioned thinking entity to a live and present one. Feelings, sensing a space of freedom without limits, naturally resurface from the depth of our unconscious. We can then access a different and unfamiliar kind of feeling: the Raw Feeling.

Raw Feelings lay at the source of our psyche where they stay as they were first experienced—pure, whole, untouched by the mind. They have not been censored or manipulated, consciously or otherwise. They have not been dissected, interpreted, or questioned. They have not yet entered the world of duality with its judgments, interpretations, and prejudices. They are in their pure original state.

However, within a fraction of a second after they are experienced, a subconscious human instinct tries to process and manipulate these raw feelings in order to avoid pain and disturbance. As a result, raw feelings often hide inside the subconscious, where they can also be fully repressed. They accumulate during our lifetime and mostly stay hidden, sometimes for a very long period of time, waiting to be found, completed, and freed.

As our intuition moves us through the process of creativity, opening us further to an innocent and nonjudgmental state, these raw feelings begin to emerge from the depths of our subconscious.

It is the tendency of our minds to impose meaning and interpretation on our feelings, weaving content and story around them. Layers of these interpretations can build up over time, covering the pure raw feelings. But our creative intuition has the power to go directly to the raw feelings and release them to move in their raw form, pushing away the prejudiced mind with all its projections as they reach toward the light.

As the raw feelings awaken, they stir and move out into our creation, finally able to complete their life journeys. They are often felt as a current of energy passing through our heart or belly. These sensations are the result of deep energies releasing and shifting in the whole body.

This leads to a pure experience of what was lost, unfinished, and unfelt. It is a delight to feel the rawness of a feeling revealing itself to consciousness and reentering the present moment, fully complete. Nothing needs to be done with it. The long-awaited guest has finally arrived. No more hiding, judging, labeling, wanting, manipulating.

Raw feelings are precious. When they stir back to life, they come with their own energy and insights. They hold the power of completion and of ending a trauma or a grief or healing a wound or ending an unacceptable situation. A feeling of goodness and potential fills the soul because what was left undone, unfelt, is on its way to integration and healing.

You do not have to tame your images.
Let them be
UNFAMILIAR, STRANGE, CROOKED, WILD,
OUTRAGEOUS AND DARING.
Do not keep your intuitive instincts in shackles.

The Thrill of Taking Risks

Don't be a slave of your thoughts and judgments;
move into your heart's fire.
Be shameless in your creation!

RUMI

The amount of freedom you experience is always
a function of how much permission you give yourself.
Become aware of that part of you
that snatches away your spontaneous tendencies
and replaces them with secondhand ideas.

Give yourself the permission to be bad, different, and audacious!
Cross the lines of the so-called acceptable, go beyond prejudices,
and free yourself from narrow codes of behavior!
Break the boundaries that surround you!
Creative freedom is calling you.

It's not a good idea to shrink or camouflage your images.
Don't let fear control you by manipulating or
covering your raw or intense images.
There is nothing to lose by being direct and bold.
Nothing is forbidden or wrong.
Do not weaken your creative potential by censoring it.

◆ ◆ ◆

Let your work not be timid; move boldly.
There is no need for reports on your progress;
they would only take away the thrill and joy of new discoveries.
The intelligence of creativity is always at work.
What does not meet your expectations is
the *most important* part of your creation
because it's purely intuitive and unplanned.

◆ ◆ ◆

If you want to feel passion in your creativity,
do not put up with the "should" and "have to."
Their presence is a sure sign
that you need to let go of your thoughts
and enter the *wildness of your soul.*

◆ ◆ ◆

No need to stay in the mind's bubble.
Unlearn perfection!

◆ ◆ ◆

Unrestrained, spontaneous expression lifts
the curtain of the unconscious
and opens you to what you do not know
about yourself and your world.
The wonder of the child in you comes back.

◆ ◆ ◆

Questions to Ponder

~ Do you want horizontal or vertical exploration?

~ What you see depends on what you do not see! How will you clear your biased eyes?

~ Are you trying to extract meaning out of appearance?

~ Are you closely watching the "I want"? Can you go beyond it?

◆ ◆ ◆

Every feeling expressed
opens a doorway to greater dimensions.

The Myth of Creative Choices

*Why are you worshipping the teapot
instead of drinking the tea?*
                                    WU HSIN

Pure Creative action is not of choosing,
deciding, or planning,
but of responding intuitively to the moment.

◆ ◆ ◆

If you think you have a choice between
two images, two colors, or two themes,
you are already in trouble.
The idea of a choice only comes when
you have left your intuition behind
and your imagination is spinning.
Intuition always *stands alone.*

◆ ◆ ◆

To ride the creative process,
you must *jump into the river of your intuition*
and meet its wild currents,
not wade in the small pools of your *changing* desires.

◆ ◆ ◆

If you believe you have a choice,
it means that you have abandoned your intuition
and that *you need to reenter your feelings*
by going beyond your preferences.

◆ ◆ ◆

but rather move your attention somewhere else in your work.
Do something simple: a dot, a line, a detail;
or ask an *impossible* question.
As you keep moving forward,
the process comes to your rescue
and guides you beyond your thinking.
The sense of a choice fades away,
and what to do next becomes obvious and heartfelt.

◆ ◆ ◆

Intuition flows through you to express,
harmonize, and integrate
the inside with the outside,
never to bring chaos or destroy
and never to ask you
to choose between possibilities.
It always points to C*ne truth, One need, One option.*

If you believe you have a choice,
choose the next move that has no choice
by getting out of the way.

With a moment of innocence,
intuition can dissolve sticky agendas
and free you from their chains.

The Flow and Cycles of Creative Energy

All life is a single event,
one moment flowing into the next naturally.
Nothing causing everything,
everything causing everything.
WU HSIN

Creative energy manifests as a flow,
punctuated by cycles, big and small.
Its heartbeat has a pulse,
a rhythm, and many seasons.
To create intuitively is to let that flow
pass through your being and move you.

Creative people are not made by hard work;
they are birthed in the fertile soil
of intuitive practice
through which they learn to act spontaneously.

◆ ◆ ◆

Believing that what you want to happen
is best for you is a misunderstanding.
Mostly, your desires are moved by vested interests
and expectations that block the natural flow of intuition.
*What you want your creation to be is irrelevant to your true
process.*

❖ ❖ ❖

Creative intuition never follows a script.
It's *fluid,*
an unpredictable response to the movement of life.

❖ ❖ ❖

In the creative process, you do not need a future.
The belief that you need to know the next step must go in order
to discover the actual potential and power of this moment.

On Stress
When stress develops in the creative process,
watch for a suddenly inflated or deflated ego.

❖ ❖ ❖

Discover what is in the way of your freedom.
Harbor a systematic refusal to indulge in preferences.
Then, space is made for creativity
to rise to the surface
naturally and instinctively.

◆ ◆ ◆

Remember that the critical voices in your head
do not know what they are talking about.
Treat them like the traffic noise outside the window.

◆ ◆ ◆

Naturally, the act of creativity aims beyond opposites.
It is creativity's basic underlying purpose
to go beyond comparisons or evaluations
and soar into unlimited space.

◆ ◆ ◆

If you become bored while you create,
you must realize that boredom is only a stern,
desperate defense against feeling your feelings.
Actually, if understood, boredom is a wake-up call.

◆ ◆ ◆

Harmony between you and your painting brings joy.
Look for the simplicity and honesty of the creative flow,
not for perfect or pleasing results.

If you think you are painting a painting,
you are mistaken!
Actually, you are traveling
through the unknowns of your life
and treading the moving waters of the moment.

◆ ◆ ◆

When you create from intuition,
you are never outside the flow of the universe.
Have faith.
Even if you do not feel inspired at this moment,
you have not been forgotten by the creative process.
You are roaming through its seasons and cycles.

◆ ◆ ◆

When you create from intuition,
you have no set direction and no place to land.
The vast world is at your feet.
You are awake, facing the present, and flowing with
life.

Questions to Ponder

~ Does the painting process move your heart and soul, or does it seem to be happening *outside of you*, like clouds passing by?

~ What do you gain from the thought that your painting is not going in the right direction?

~ Do you think you can know what needs to happen next? In which compartment of your mind are you looking?

~ If you cannot trust the rhythm of nature born from your own essence, what can you trust?

◆ ◆ ◆

Loops in Creativity

The mind is always looking for distraction, entertainment, clever ideas, or complicated scenarios. In creating within the thinking field, the mind believes it has found what it was searching for and, for a time, becomes engaged and satisfied, feeding on its desired food.

Unfortunately, after a while that kind of creativity is bound to backfire and bring the person into what I call a *loop*.

Loops are places where people seem to turn in circles, not feeling really inspired and just pleased enough to keep going. This happens when the understanding and practice of creativity are not fully realized and the thinking process still controls their doings, unaware that they are free to roam into the mystery and explore the truly unknowns of creativity.

The only way to get out of a creative loop is to discover how to *move beyond thinking*: how *not* to follow the thoughts that are trying to direct, control, and feed the experience of creativity. People who are trapped in the loop need to realize that for creative intuition to bloom, a full letting go, a full surrender to Being is necessary. Then and then only, intuition rises and carries the creative process to truly new grounds that are refreshing and revitalizing and have *nothing* to do with their old way of creating.

◆ ◆ ◆

Loops take place when creative liveliness disappears.
When you are in a loop, you might be content enough,

but you are on the edge of boredom.
yet not knowing what else to do, you keep going,
sometimes for a very long time,
never truly satisfied or dissatisfied.

◆ ◆ ◆

Loops start when you pick mental themes or goals
that have emotional overtones and get hooked there,
believing you are following your intuition,
when actually
you are following your head, not your heart.

◆ ◆ ◆

Loops happen when you cannot stop
using a mental process as a tool to create.
The way out of a loop is
to jump into the non-thinking creative space
and experience the *dizziness* of facing the creative void.

◆ ◆ ◆

You do not need to enhance your creations.
What you deeply want is to experience the fullness
and beauty of creative surrender
and feel astonishment at what grows
spontaneously and incessantly out of you.

◆ ◆ ◆

Losing degrees of inspiration
and finding them again is quite natural.
It is the breathing in and out of the creative flow
that moves naturally through its cycles.

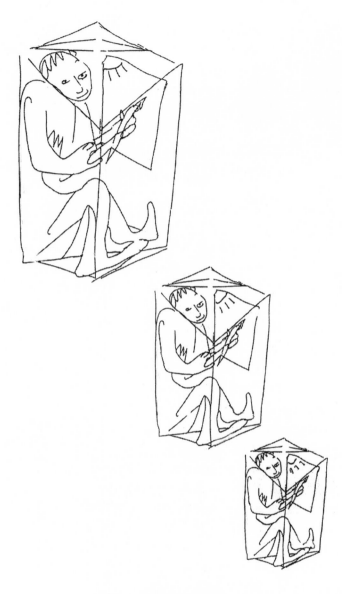

It is NOT what
you have let go of
that is important,
it is what you have NOT let go of!

Who Is Painting?
Who Are You When You Create?

To inhabit the creative flow, with its pulse and cycles,
you need to let go, time after time,
of what you are not!
That is the final test.

M. C.

Spontaneous creativity is powerful;
it can break the boundaries of
who you think you are
and free you from your many costumes.

Humans have a tendency to hide their true selves
and to sometimes create in order to impress others
or to embellish their self-images.
It is essential that these patterns become conscious
and watched during the creative process
lest you paint from a theater role.

By clinging to your creations
and using them to become a different person,
you are *fragmenting* yourself.
Then, the broken pieces of your self
drain the elixir of creativity.

◆ ◆ ◆

Pure creativity naturally breaks
your self-identification with particular types.
It delivers you from layers of models and restrictions.
By becoming aware of this role-playing and its limitations,
you discover *who* is left underneath it all.
If your only purpose in painting
is to "become an artist,"
that is all you will get.

◆ ◆ ◆

When you create, the best route is
to let yourself be fully who you are.
Discover the amazing safety and
joyful potential of an open and willing self.

◆ ◆ ◆

In pure creativity, every brushstroke undoes, erases,
and dissolves who you thought you were.
It is the deeper purpose of creativity:
to free you from the prison of self-definition.
Who creates then? What is left when self-identification is gone?

◆ ◆ ◆

By freeing you from old conditioning,
creativity erodes your personal will.
As it happens, the field of creative exploration widens,
bringing a new breath of awareness into your life.
There, you face the potent question, Who is painting?
Nobody but *you* can answer that ancient question.

Questions to Ponder

~ Why paint like someone else? Why would anyone want to paint like another?

~ Who is painting? What is the energy that makes you move? What is its source, its identity?

~ When everything flows without friction or pressure, who creates?

~ When there is no one working toward a special goal, what is left at the core of your being?

~ Who am I? What am I?

◆ ◆ ◆

As water goes down the mountain, intuitive painters find their way by following the current of their own *awakened* wisdom.

You never need to look for ideas;
just inhabit the feelings of the moment.
Reenter yourself and all will flow spontaneously.

Meditation and the Creative Process
The Non-Thinking Creativity

To enter the creative process is to practice direct action, the non-thinking action; it is a blessed state of **non-doing**. *Pure creativity is meditation in action.* When I ask my students to paint or create without thinking, they first feel lost and wonder why not use what they spent their whole life developing—a sharp mind that knows how to organize and plan.

They often do not want to, or just think they cannot stop using their most developed tool: their sophisticated thinking.

Meditators are more used to letting their thoughts go, but often when they are asked to create from intuition, they discover how deeply conditioned and attached to acting from thinking they still are. They realize how precious a practice of intuitive creativity can become because it shows them how their feelings are prisoners of their thoughts.

Creation beyond thinking offers a means to enter the moment and explore the unknown.

◆ ◆ ◆

Make peace with difficult times.
Ultimately, they will open a gateway to ecstasy.

Going beyond the Obvious
Entering the Mystery

True innocence requires
the willingness to be hurt,
to be wrong,
to be awed and out of control.
True innocence is the doorway to the eternal.
                                    WU HSIN

Creative intuition is a killer of concepts!
Watch it undermine mental strongholds
and erase the rigid prejudices of the psyche,
endlessly revealing the essence of your being.

◆ ◆ ◆

The practice of pure creativity reconnects us
with the flow of life and its mysterious movements—
flow that has been unaltered and inhibited
by fears, beliefs, and secondhand knowledge.
When creativity is rediscovered in its purest form,
the process takes you naturally
to the exploration of spiritual dimensions.

The eyes of perception are hooked
by *particular stories and beliefs.*
With the practice of intuition,
they get out of the way and
allow the heart and soul
to burst into their amazing powers of revelation.
Your inner vision, then, can see far, anew, and beyond.

◆ ◆ ◆

Art process is meditation.
The creative process guides you to act
from a *non-dual place,*
from a non-thinking place,
revealing the hidden
and the sacred from within.

◆ ◆ ◆

The creative process, if you flow with it,
reveals the many dimensions of consciousness.
Forever going beyond
what has been seen and understood,
it has no limit.

◆ ◆ ◆

Destroying false ideas about yourself
brings about liveliness and truth.
These two qualities are the deepest aspects
of every creative moment,
the most significant of creativity's offerings.

◆ ◆ ◆

While passing through you,
intuitive energy dissolves
the accumulated remains of your life,
whether conscious or unconscious.
Its kind and transcendent presence
cleanses and heals.

◆ ◆ ◆

Be gentle and loving to yourself;
let yourself be as you are when you create,
and your spirit will guide you and blossom.

◆ ◆ ◆

Wisdom's giving of the principles is
the cornerstone of all creative power.

◆ ◆ ◆

The sacred energy that moves and inspires your creativity
through its many phases can be called love.
When you discover that hidden truth,
you can give yourself to it without restraint,
knowing that love works always
for the awakening of your true nature.

◆ ◆ ◆

Painting must continue until the disappearance
of the painter.

The Transcendent Power of Pure Creativity
From Insights to Revelations

A few days ago, all of a sudden, fireworks exploded in my head.

Eureka! After fifty years of giving my life to creativity, I had the most transcendent revelation. It happened in Taos, New Mexico, before a workshop while I was exploring my raw feelings and the creative instinct. As fast as a lightning, I was suddenly connecting the dots of understanding I had gathered over fifty years.

Many years ago, I had seen that creativity was not just an individual doing but was moved by universal energy; I also saw that there was a definite flow to it, a flow that had intelligence, benevolence, and spirit. In the following decades, I came upon many more findings, but recently, while in Taos preparing my long yearly workshop, I suddenly watched all my findings connect themselves easily, simply, and obviously to reveal to me how deeply creativity works. I marveled at it and felt an immense gratitude for the profound clarity and beauty of such vision, the sacredness of it, and the perfection of the gift.

Years ago, I painted an image of my mother, feeling the discomfort of an unfinished relationship. In the midst of painting her, all of a sudden I saw my mother as a link in the human chain of birth and death. I saw her as a lively, mysterious being, living on many planes of existence and spirit. I perceived her as a totally different entity in an entirely new context. The impact on me was astounding.

My little problems on Earth became so tiny that they dissolved instantly when facing the immensity of Being. Without a warning, I had stepped out of my usual way of seeing and moved into the great mystery of life with its spiritual and metaphysical dimensions.

During the years that followed, the same kinds of experiences often happened to me while painting and sustained my passion and my trust in the creative process. I could sense that painting would keep showing me glimpses of truths. I looked at my practice of creativity as an unfolding, mystical journey, yet it still held secrets from me. *How and why could such transformations and such perceptions in other dimensions be possible?*

That recent day in Taos, I suddenly became clear on how the intuitive process works and affects consciousness. I realized that when the feelings are untouched, unmanipulated, and undefined— **when they are in *their raw form*—**their connection with the mystery of life and its many levels are live and active. No repressions are present, no denial, no fears blocking them, no projection covering them; they are readily available. So when raw feelings arise from the unconscious, they naturally carry with them the context of life, the unknown, the other planes of awareness, and the other dimensions of spirit and bring them to consciousness.

The whole of reality is always there, but as humans we mostly are blind to it. But when an old experience in its raw form rises freely in the creative vortex, it brings with it the context of the original state of reality that was missed or ignored. Creative energy uncovers and reveals what we could *not see or realize at the time* and leads us toward an expanded reality, which holds a beauty so intense that at times it is hardly bearable.

This is the great gift of creativity, the gold mine. The discovery is not just in the recovered feelings, but also in their **connections**

with the whole of life. The power of intuition is not only in expressing the feelings we have created out of our experiences, but also in bringing what is around these feelings, in them, through them, and from different planes of consciousness.

Creativity offers a new way of looking at our lives. Its revelations can be astonishing. They appear unexpectedly from *a level of reality that had become unconscious to us.* This is why the focus should never be put on the interpretation or explanation of our visible creations but on surrendering to the spontaneous movement of intuition. It also explains why new insights sometimes have nothing to do with the content of our creation and yet are stimulated by it.

The flow of pure creativity moves from a place of *nonduality.* Creativity gives us what we really need: not only the option to heal and integrate our feelings but also the power to expand our consciousness and awareness. This is the truest, deepest purpose of pure creative intuition. Pure creativity can move us from insights to revelations, from the known to the unknown and into the unknowable.

Do not try to please your students.

They deserve more.

Principles of Creativity for Teachers

Too much time is squandered on what was
and what could be,
leaving only table scraps for what is.
WU HSIN

When painters find their creative passion, they often feel eager to lead others on the same path. Since the intuition in teaching comes from the same place as in painting, they already have a base for teaching. **Their teaching must not come from rational thinking or memory but from their intuition**.

Creative teachers act as guides and catalysts, not as authorities; they have no agenda or designed path for their students. This sharing of creativity is a learning journey for teachers and students alike. They know creativity from the inside, and, as they practice, new creative principles are constantly revealed to them and understood.

Here are some of those principles:

Teaching creativity can never be stereotyped.
Teachers are birthed through their own creative work,
not groomed to memorize techniques and rules.

◆ ◆ ◆

Teachers can convey only what they have experienced.
They must test their teaching on themselves.
Do they practice what they teach?

◆ ◆ ◆

Teachers' spontaneity and freedom of expression are essential.
If teachers prepare and calculate every interaction,
they are prisoners of their preconceived ideas
and are applying stale recipes.

◆ ◆ ◆

Critiques and judgments are felt by others even when not verbalized.
Since we can't help but project unconsciously
how we judge our students and their work,
it is crucial to become aware of our projections.

◆ ◆ ◆

Teachers do not need to resolve their students' problems or creative blocks.
They only need to guide students to understand how creativity works and how to find answers there.

◆ ◆ ◆

On the necessity of being fully honest
If you do not act like yourself when you teach,
when will you do so?
Where else would that need be more crucial?

◆ ◆ ◆

On teachers' inspiration
If you think that what you are is not enough to teach,
where are you going to find what you need?

◆ ◆ ◆

On teachers' joy
Newness, surprises, and adventure are the *playground* of creative teachers. Find that joy!

◆ ◆ ◆

Teaching to enhance your self-image is not an option.
If the purpose for teaching is to identify oneself
with the label of *teacher,* the point has been missed.
Teaching creativity is *never* about
strengthening your self-image.

◆ ◆ ◆

True teaching comes out of what is real in the teacher.
Teachers must jump into the stream of life with their students
and follow the currents of their intuition,
not their thoughts.

◆ ◆ ◆

The belief that one needs to change to become a good teacher
is a false belief.
There is no need to become someone special to teach creativity;
You only need to have integrity.

◆ ◆ ◆

No hierarchy in teaching
Watch the teacher hierarchy in yourself.
See the temptation of power
that might be hiding with external good intentions.
Discover that there are many layers of
holding on to authority and clever ways to use it.

On the dangers of teacher's flattery
Do not fall into the temptation to
judge or flatter yourself about your teaching.
It cannot be done without the risk of *weakening or blocking your intuition.*
It is best not to pay attention to compliments. Let them go.

On not needing to know the next step
Never force anything in a student's work.
The desire to know the next step must dry up and go.
Listen carefully to the next spontaneous inspiration,
the next instinct, the next impulse,
even a tiny one.
Let the next step surprise you again and again.

On challenging students to be real
Remember that to teach creativity is to ask students something
very difficult, something that during the rest of their lives
they avoid carefully and struggle with;
not protecting themselves and being fully who they are.

◆ ◆ ◆

To teach creativity is to never use a script.
Just the opposite, it is stepping out of
all stereotype roles and plans.

◆ ◆ ◆

Always teach creativity as...
　　　　　self-expression...
　　　　　　　　　self-discovery, and...
　　　　　　　　　　　　　self-exploration.

Questions to Ponder

On teachers' struggles
~ Who is fighting whom? Are you fighting your students or yourself or both?

◆ ◆ ◆

On the automatic need to evaluate your teaching
~ What does the mind gain from the thought that your teaching is good or bad? Think about it.

◆ ◆ ◆

Listening is not just hearing words.
~ Can you believe what your students are telling you?
~ Do you listen to words *only*, or are all your senses open and eager to perceive the student?

◆ ◆ ◆

Stepping into the moment
~ The first thing to establish is whether you are coming from a place of surrendering to your intuition, or whether you are in control, using a plan or a strategy.

◆ ◆ ◆

◆ ◆ ◆

∼ Are you inside the **creative field** with your students?

◆ ◆ ◆

∼ Are you looking at **techniques** and **agendas** as unwanted crutches?

◆ ◆ ◆

Teachers' Occasional Challenges

A caged bird is not freed merely by opening the door.
Until the fear of the unknown subsides,
until the desire arises to fly away
the bird remains where it is
Preferring the known to the unknown.

WU HSIN

Make peace with discomfort; welcome it!
Discomfort has come to teach you.
Listen to it and *dare to be yourself.*
Discomfort will guide you
to a new place of harmony with your students.

◆ ◆ ◆

What you are is quite enough.
To truly teach or create you only have
to dare taking the risk to be yourself.

◆ ◆ ◆

On rejecting agendas and techniques
See that you only get stuck or frustrated
when you have agendas for yourself or your students.

◆ ◆ ◆

Experience teachers' traps
when inner freedom is lost,
you become slaves of teachers' appearances
and of stereotyped expectations.
You become mechanical in your teaching
and soon create boredom in your students.

◆ ◆ ◆

What pleases you holds you back.
Watch your pride when your student has a breakthrough.
Do not think you did it!
Remember that it happened through
the magic of the creative process, not by you.

◆ ◆ ◆

Read the signs of teachers' stress.
They point to a lack of presence and aliveness
probably due to an inflated self-image.
Stress is a wake-up call.
Our minds might be running the show,
encased in good or bad, success or failure.

◆ ◆ ◆

Drop the teacher's role; be human.
It's so refreshing to drop the teaching role
that thinks it knows better and feels
superior to the students.
Let your creativity grow in your soul,
your heart, and your guts beyond any comparison.

◆ ◆ ◆

Contact with the student.
The point of contact with intuition is
the point of contact with life,
with you, and with your students.

◆ ◆ ◆

Teaching is about your students, not about you.
Focus on the students, not your performance.
Don't rehearse. Teach from where you are.
The more you are caught in yourself,
the more you are separate from others.

◆ ◆ ◆

Teacher listening
Do not believe what your students' mouths are saying.
You must listen to the whole of them.
Open your inner ears!

A teacher is a mirror, not an authority.

The Call of Creativity Answered

When the creative principles are embraced and understood, creators of all kinds find inspiration that guides them to joyfully sail through the ups and downs of their processes and explore the unknown.

The creative process becomes a true adventure and an endless exploration into the mystery of life. It soon becomes quite clear that the creative process works for the expansion of our being and spirit, taking us back to our essence.

We open to unexpected waves of revelations and insights and let them rise, bloom, and give fruit. These creative waves follow the golden thread of intuition, leading us to what we need to express, release, and realize.

Creative passion is born, and creativity can fulfill its powerful potential and deepest purpose.

Afterword
Making Intuitive Creativity Simple

When I first discovered spontaneous painting, my passion to create exploded in such a way that I could never find enough time for it.

This is when I found out that I could draw whenever painting was not easily available: when traveling, commuting on the Paris metro, visiting friends, and having to bear these four- to five-hour family gatherings. Drawing helped me escape boring situations and delight in my creative passion.

I used to carry with me a little blank book and a pen wherever I went, but when I found myself without them I would use anything at hand—a napkin, the back of any brochure, or a piece of newspaper—and always managed to draw and keep the river of creativity flowing in me no matter what. I felt so much joy, fulfillment, and comfort watching my pen trace all sorts of surprising shapes and images. Drawing seemed to bring peace to me, and I noticed that my mind became more silent and friendly to me whenever I did it. At times, some hidden feelings arose and flowed out of me much to my surprise; at other times my perceptions shifted to another level of Being.

These drawings were born with their own lives and evolved on their own. It was fascinating that they seemed to appear without asking for my opinions or preferences. I plunged in the mystery of life, and I felt safe and immensely grateful.

It was so simple; all I needed was a pen and paper. I worked on each drawing as long as I felt drawn to it; I wanted them to use me fully before moving to the next one, always eager and wondering about the hidden unknown. I completed each drawing as if it was the natural thing to do, out of respect for this mysterious process.

Instinctively, I made no judgments, no evaluations, or interpretations. I was only responding to the inner urge, trusting and curious. My secret life was unfolding, and I decided to never show these works to anyone. It was a wonderful and unexpected freedom, a gift of space and permission.

Drawing touched the same freedom I had found in painting. Though I noticed the color of painting adds a subtle dimension to the movement of intuition, I still had many experiences drawing that had the same quality and depth as painting.

I was on a journey, and every step, whether painting or drawing, took me to that mysterious adventure.

◆ ◆ ◆

Appendix

Drawing Suggestions

And How to Keep Your Intuition Flowing with Pen and Paper while Exploring the Creative Unknown.

Drawing is a very practical option when painting is not possible, such as when traveling, when painting is inconvenient, or when the body is tired and needs a rest. It is also possible to draw outside while enjoying the fresh air and nice weather, in a café atmosphere, or anywhere comfortable and a little private.

To draw, I recommend using whatever size of blank paper book is convenient for you to easily carry. Experiment to see what suits you. I personally enjoy working in a little sketchbook—you can find many different types in art stores—this way all the drawings stay neatly together, and they are easy to carry in a handbag. Any ink pen will work wonderfully, but if you are attracted to a brush pen or felt pen or colored pencil or crayons, I encourage you to follow that urge and experiment. A black pen is a basic requirement, but having a red pen as a companion is good for contrast. Ink pens have many colors and tip sizes that allow different thickness of lines and allow you to explore the medium.

- It is important to start **without plans or themes**. You do not need to be in a special state or mood to create. Start where you are. You have all you need inside yourself when you make a spontaneous drawing.

- Then, you go one step at a time, **right into the unknown**. At times you might just draw dots or simple lines, at other times a very full surface, or you might reinvent images with spontaneous proportions and colors. There are no rules and no limitations; *spontaneity and intuition guide your hand.* Let it all be. You can delight in discovering the infinite possibilities of lines and tones that can combine in amazing ways.

- **If you feel restless and bored,** I recommend that you still keep going. These feelings are a sign that you must add a new ingredient: CARE. It's an important time, a time to slow down and sense your true needs, a time to *care* for your work; often you find a small detail that might look insignificant and unnecessary to the mind but that might propel you in a new direction and discovery. Do not be fooled! Caring is a magical ingredient that destroys the tendency of the mind to control and severely censor the final product, ripping it from its liveliness.

- **Give full respect** to what is done and create with innocence. If not, restlessness might increase and eventually stop the intuitive flow. The remedy to a lack of inspiration is always the same: *face the restlessness and do not give up.* You will be surprised by the birth of new images or shapes seemingly coming out of nowhere, rising from far away, deep from the unconscious or subconscious. Unexpected images will pass through you bringing bursts of new energy. Suddenly, you will realize that the restlessness has dissolved and a keen interest in your work has appeared. The deeper the images are buried in you, the more time it might take for fresh bursts of the new to appear, but the more powerful and insightful your creation will be.

This approach cannot fail because **by not listening to the pull toward simple pleasure** (the indulgent part of you), you are walking right back into yourself and freeing the caged feelings and perceptions that were unknown to you a moment before.

- Draw as long as it feels natural to you. If you do not finish the drawing, pick it up at the next opportunity.

It is important to avoid interpreting and jumping to conclusions about the meaning of the drawings in your life; just wait for insights to come in their own time, and they will bring their wisdom and liveliness to you when ready. As you let go of the temptation to control, you are opening a gateway into the mystery of life and beyond.

- The key to intuitive drawing is to not to be seduced by visions of what you think will make you happy or satisfied. You must become aware of that ingrained human pattern that wants to control creativity, and you need to see that *there is another way:* welcoming what comes naturally and spontaneously—the non-thinking creativity.

As you become open and vulnerable to what is natural—which most of the time does not match what you expect—the door of pure intuition opens and frees images and colors that are inside you all the way down in your soul. Your soul, spirit, or heart recognizes that energy, and your being expands as a wrinkled cloth does when it is stretched. Rejoice in the amazing experience of moving through new perceptions, feelings, and sensations.

- **Keep drawing**, go one step at a time, listen to your intuition, and respond subtly or boldly to its lively and changing currents. Like a tunnel opening to the light, you will soon find yourself traveling into new lands beyond your familiar expectations.

- **There is no need to grab anything,** no need to put words to your experience. It would be like pouring water on a hot fire. Stay in the humble place of vulnerability and receptivity.

As you go on, your creativity takes you to new levels, and you need to keep going no matter the roughness or strangeness of the journey. It is absolutely important to continue despite your mind's comments and hesitations.

- For each new start, you need to go back to a state of innocence and vulnerability. With each step, follow the unknown current, the mysterious path, and welcome its intuitive gift without judgment.

- Then, listen more and more closely to catch anything in the field of the intuitive unknown. Just like a detective finding clues through pure attention and openness, you might find little marks, dots, colors, or images. Use anything that asks to be there without forcing any of it.

- Make sure the drawing is finished before you let it go, even if there is a lot in it. Remember that finishing is not adding but responding with care and subtleties, naturally. It is also preparing on a subtle level the next creative birth.

- When finished, you are ready to start your next drawing and go on your creative adventure. Your new work will bring you to an ever-deeper level of feelings and realizations. Often you might be surprised to watch unconscious material freeing itself and bringing new perceptions and new consciousness to your life and Being.

The call of creativity is being answered.

◆ ◆ ◆

Acknowledgments

I want to give my most heartfelt thanks to my good friend and fellow teacher, Anna Billings, who offered constant support during the making of this book. My heartfelt thanks as well go to Cherie Ray, Bonnie Cohen, Linda Stich and Zoe Hill for their care and love in helping me during the completion of this book. I am also grateful to my editors, Sue Mann and Sasa Gyoker, and to George Rosenfeld for designing the cover.
And I have much loving gratitude for all my students who have inspired me for so many years.

For books or workshop information,
videos, audio, or catalogs,
or to be put on the mailing list,
visit Michele's website, www.michelecassou.com.

About the Author

Michele Cassou, a passionate painter and teacher, is the creator of an original method of creative painting. She was born and raised in southern France. As a young adult, she moved to Paris, where she studied law, literature, and art. Inspired by watching children paint, she discovered a way to express herself spontaneously and without the need for conventional training.

A unique approach to creativity grew out of her many years of "just painting for herself."

She is known internationally for her groundbreaking work in freeing the creative potential and exploring the spiritual dimensions of the creative process. She has taught thousands of students over more than four decades. She currently conducts workshops in the San Francisco area in different venues, at the Esalen

Institute in Big Sur, California, and at the Mabel Dodge Luhan House in Taos, New Mexico.

A passionate artist, she has painted thousands of paintings, authored many books, and produced videos and CDs of her work. Though educated in Paris, she has lived most of her life in California, where she continues to paint and write.
With the creative people who worked with her, she founded in 2015, in Marin, California, a non profit organization called the Cassou Institute for Creative Freedom.

Made in the USA
Middletown, DE
21 December 2019